W9-BKM-032

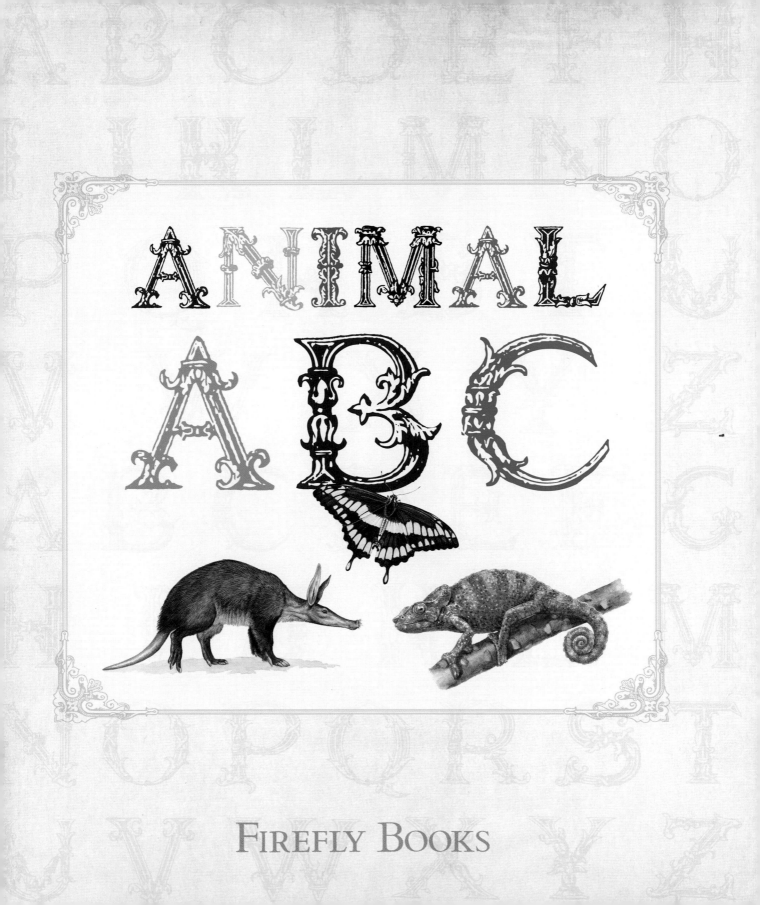

ANIMAL
ABC

FIREFLY BOOKS

A is for alligator

aardvark

B **b**

is for butterflies

C c

is for cheetah

camels

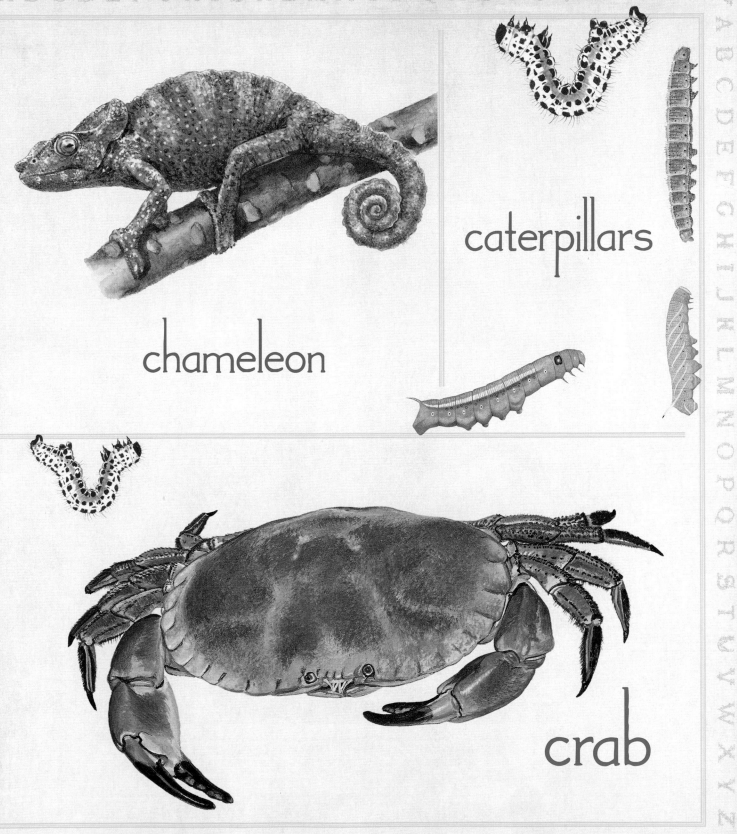

caterpillars

chameleon

crab

D d

is for duck

dolphin

dragonfly

E e

is for eagle

elephant

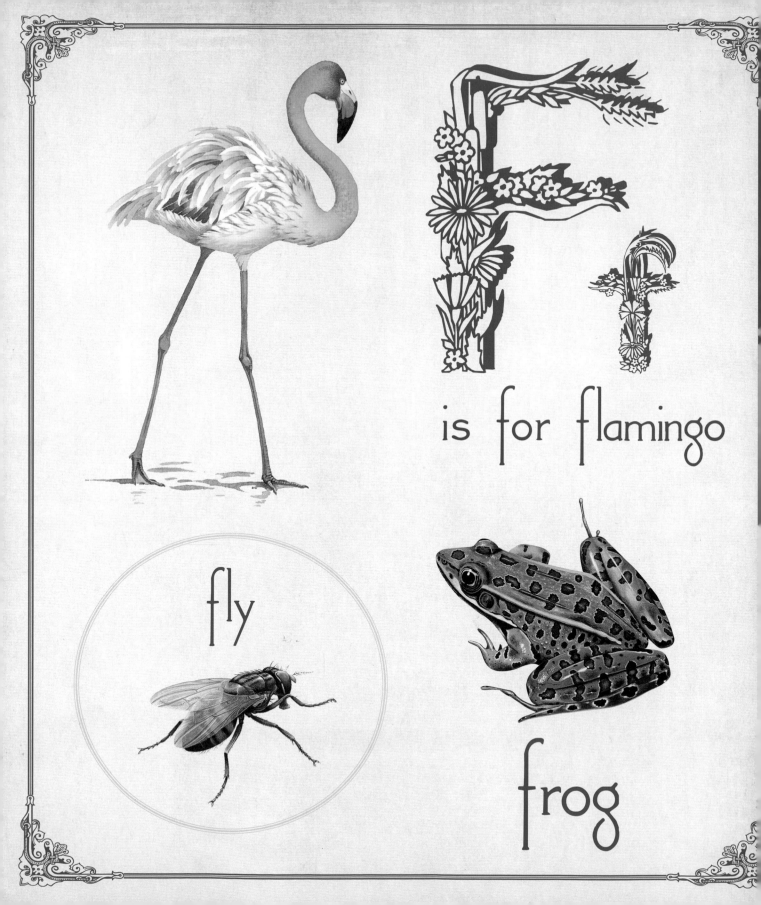

is for flamingo

fly

frog

is for giraffe

goose

grasshopper

Hh is for hedgehog

hummingbird

hippopotamus

is for ibis

iguana

impala

Jj

is for jellyfish

jaguar

koala

kingfisher

K is for kangaroo

L is for leopard

lemur

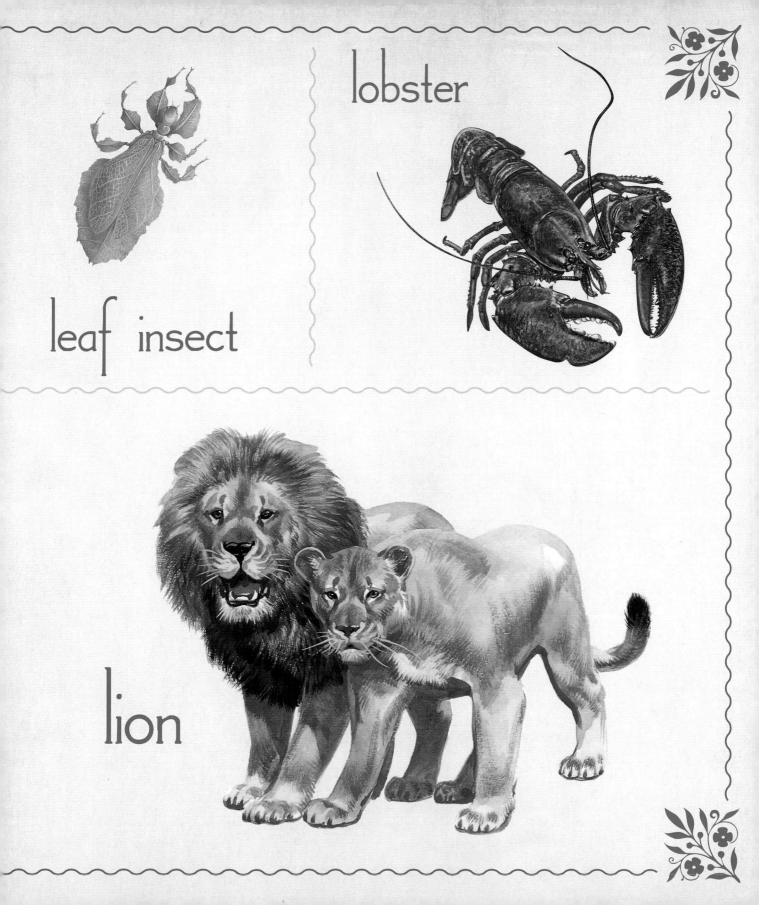

leaf insect

lobster

lion

Mm

is for macaw

mantis

monkeys

Nn

is for newts

narwhal

O is for orangutan

ostrich

octopus

is for peacock

python

piranha

penguin

panda

platypus

Q q

is for quetzal

quelea

quail

R r

is for raccoon

rabbit

robin

is for swan

squirrel

starfish

salamander

Tt

is for tortoise

tarantula

toucan

tuna

U is for

umbrella bird

uakari

is for vulture

vole

viper

W w

is for woodpecker

walrus

warthog

whales

X x is for X-ray fish

Y is for yak

Z z

is for zebra

zorilla

zander

A FIREFLY BOOK

Published by Firefly Books Ltd. 2014

First printing

Publisher Cataloging-in-Publication Data (U.S.)

Martin, Susi.
Animal ABC / Susi Martin.
[32] pages : col. photos. ; cm.
Summary: An introduction to the alphabet and the animal kingdom through illustrations of aardvarks and alligators to zebras.
ISBN: 978-1-77085-456-7
1.Alphabet - Juvenile literature. 2. English language – Alphabet – Juvenile literature. 3. Animals – Juvenile literature. I. Title.
421.1 [E] dc23 PE1155.M368 2014

Library and Archives Canada Cataloguing in Publication

Martin, Susi, author
    Animal ABC / Susi Martin.
ISBN 978-1-77085-456-7 (bound)
    1. English language—Alphabet—Juvenile literature. 2. Alphabet—Juvenile literature. 3. Picture books for children. I. Title.
PE1155.M36 2014   j421'.1   C2014-901868-1

Published in the United States by
Firefly Books (U.S.) Inc.
P.O. Box 1338, Ellicott Station
Buffalo, New York 14205

Published in Canada by
Firefly Books Ltd.
50 Staples Avenue, Unit 1
Richmond Hill, Ontario L4B 0A7

Designed and edited by Tall Tree Ltd

Printed in China